KIDS'

HALLOWEEN PARTY

Executive Producers: Kim Mitzo Thompson, Karen Mitzo Hilderbrand
Audio Track Programming: David Paglisotti
Author: Ken Carder
Book Design: Matthew Van Zomeren
Pumpkin Carving Patterns: David Schimmell

Twin Sisters Productions
4710 Hudson Drive
Stow, OH 44224 USA
www.twinsisters.com
1-800-248-8946

Bug Blood

Thirsting for something really creepy?

You'll need:
- Two 10-oz packages of frozen strawberries, defrosted
- One 6-oz can of lemonade concentrate, thawed
- One quart of ginger ale
- Two Cups of raisins

Mix the strawberries and lemonade concentrate in a blender until smooth and thick. Slowly add ginger ale to the strawberry-lemonade mixture. Pour the drink into a punch bowl, then stir in the raisins and pretend they're tasty "floating bugs!"

Slime Juice

You'll need:
- 6-oz package of blue powdered drink mix
- 12-oz can orange juice concentrate
- 1-gallon water

Mix together the orange juice and powdered drink mix, add water, stir and watch the beverage turn green.

Here is another tasty disgusting option:

You'll need:
- 2 packages of lime gelatin (3-oz size)
- 1-½ Cups water, boiling
- 6-oz frozen Limeade
- 2 Cups water
- Green food coloring
- 10-oz Club soda or carbonated water

Prepare the lime gelatin according to the package directions. Carefully pour the mixture into a 9-inch square pan and chill about three hours, until firm. In a large pitcher, combine the limeade, remaining water and food coloring to turn the drink bright green. Chill the drink. When the gelatin is set, cut out strips or small shapes using cookie cutters. To serve, add club soda or carbonate water to the limeade and pour over ice. Put a lime gelatin shape in each glass.

Boiling Witch's Cauldron

You'll need:
- A plastic witch's cauldron from your nearest Halloween supply store
- Frozen lemonade or other drink mix
- 2 Two-liter lemon-lime or ginger ale sodas
- Cut up fresh fruit: watermelon, strawberries, melons, oranges, grapes
- Grape powdered drink mix
- Optional: plastic bones, spiders, bats
- Optional: dry ice—used only with adult supervision

In the clean plastic witch's cauldron, prepare the frozen drink mix according to package instructions. Add the lemon-lime soda or ginger ale. Add the cut-up fruit. Darken the mixture with grape powdered drink mix. For added effect, add plastic bones, eyeballs, bats, spiders or other ghoulish toys. Only with adult supervision, add dry ice for the boiling effect and to have "steam" rolling over the edges.

Remove the dry ice before serving.

Sewer Slurpies

Disgusting? Yes, but a tasty ice cream slurpy beverage!

You'll need:
- Chocolate chip ice cream
- Chocolate syrup
- Club soda
- Large glasses
- Straws
- Spoons

Let the ice cream sit at room temperature until it's easy to scoop. Fill tall glasses about half full with the ice cream goop. Squeeze several tablespoons of chocolate syrup into each glass. Slowly fill glasses with club soda and serve with a straw and long spoon.

Vampire's Blood Shake

You'll need:
- 2 Cups plain yogurt
- ½ Teaspoon vanilla extract
- 1 Package frozen strawberries or raspberries, thawed
- Ice cubes
- 1 Pint strawberry ice cream

Mix yogurt, vanilla, and berries in the blender. Pour into tall glasses over ice cubes, or chill. Top with a big spoonful of strawberry ice cream.

Gruesome Brew

A spicy hot drink to warm little goblins.

You'll need:
- ½-cup lemon juice
- 1 Quart apple cider
- 5 Cloves
- 1 teaspoon nutmeg
- 2 Cinnamon sticks

Mix lemon juice and cider in a saucepan. Put the cloves, nutmeg and cinnamon in a tea ball and add to cider. Bring the mixture to a boil over low heat and simmer for 5 - 10 minutes. Cool slightly, remove tea ball, and serve. The brew may also be served cold.

Worms In The Mud

Eat dirt? Eat worms? Sure you can—with this tasty chocolate pudding treat.

You'll need:
- Instant chocolate pudding mix
- Gummy worms
- Chocolate graham crackers

Follow the directions on the box of the pudding mix; make sure you stir it enough to get rid of the lumps. Put it in the refrigerator to set. When the pudding is set, crumble up some graham crackers and mix them into the pudding. Next, stir in some gummy worms, making sure they are covered in pudding. Divide the pudding into four dishes, crumble some more graham crackers on top, and add a couple of worms!

Green Eye Pie

How many eyes are in this pie?

You'll need:
- Green grapes
- Whipped topping or sour cream
- Prepared graham cracker pie crust
- 2 Tablespoons brown sugar

In a bowl combine 2 cups of washed and dried green grapes and ½-cup of whipped topping (or sour cream). Pour into the prepared graham cracker pie crust. Chill. Sprinkle with brown sugar before serving.

Skull Cakes

Serve these long-lost human skulls to your guests!

You'll need:
- Cupcakes in liners
- Marshmallows
- White frosting
- Mints
- Chocolate chips
- Slivered almonds

Cut the marshmallows in half. (Kitchen shears dipped in confectioner's sugar keeps the marshmallows from sticking.) Pull each cupcake liner away and tuck half a marshmallow between the paper and the cupcake. Frost the cupcake and marshmallow to create a skull. Add mints or chocolate chips for eyes. Use slivered almonds for teeth.

Chocolate-Covered Bugs

Tasty little insects are so much fun!

You'll need:
- Red-licorice whips
- Soft caramel candies
- Chocolate chips
- Optional: Colored sprinkles, candies, coconut sliced Almonds
- Baking sheet
- Waxed Paper

First, cut the licorice whips into small pieces and set them aside. Unwrap the caramels and flatten each one into a small oval with your hands. Press the small pieces of licorice onto each of the flattened caramels to make bug legs. Top each bug with a second caramel and seal together by pressing the edges. Put each bug on a baking sheet lined with waxed paper.

Melt the chocolate chips in a microwave-safe bowl. Microwave on High about 1 minute. Stir. Then microwave on High 1 minute longer. Remove the chocolate from the microwave and stir until melted. Spoon melted chocolate over each candy. Decorate the bugs with nuts, candies, sprinkles, or coconut.

Spider Guts Cake

Slice into this gooey cake for a disgusting surprise!

You'll need:
- 1 Basic cake mix
- 1 Package of green gelatin, prepared according to package directions
- Black frosting–available at craft supply stores or make your own by adding blue food coloring to chocolate frosting
- Black licorice sticks or whips
- Large green gumdrops

Mix the cake batter according to package directions. Bake it in two metal bowls —one bowl larger than the other. Once the cakes have baked and cooled, remove them from the mold. To make the spider's body, cut the larger cake in half horizontally. Scoop out a hole in each half. Fill the hole with the green gelatin. Put both halves of the larger cake back together. Frost it black and arrange on a serving platter, adding the legs and eyes. When the cake is cut into, it will ooze green guts!

Kitty Litter Cake

Imagine serving invited guests your kitty's dirty litter for dessert!

You'll need
- 1 Spice cake mix
- 1 White cake mix
- 1 Package of white sandwich cookies
- Green food coloring
- 12 Small, rounded chocolate stick rolls
- 1 Package vanilla pudding mix
- 1 New kitty litter box
- 1 New "Pooper Scooper" utensil

Prepare the cake mixes and bake according to the package directions. Prepare the pudding mix and chill until ready to assemble. Crumble white sandwich cookies in small batches in blender. Set aside all but about ½-cup. Add a few drops green food coloring to the ½-cup of cookie crumbs, and mix using a fork. When cooled to room temperature, crumble both cakes into a large bowl. Toss with half the remaining cookie crumbs and the chilled pudding. Gently combine. Line new, clean kitty litter box with plastic wrap. Spread the cake and cookie mixture into the litter box. Heat several unwrapped rounded chocolate stick rolls in a microwave safe dish until soft and pliable. Shape the ends of the chocolate so they are no longer blunt, curving slightly. Bury the chocolate treats in the "litter" mixture. Sprinkle the other half of cookie crumbs over top. Scatter the green cookie crumbs lightly over the top—to represent the chlorophyll in kitty litter. Heat remaining chocolate stick rolls in the microwave until almost melted. Scrape them on top of the cake and sprinkle with cookie crumbs. Serve the dessert with a new "Pooper Scooper"—the small shovel-like utensil used for sifting kitty litter.

Dead Finger Cookies

Cookies give new meaning to the term "finger food."

You'll need:
- Cookie dough
- Almonds

Put refrigerated sugar cookie dough in a large plastic storage bag. Cut a "finger-size" corner off the bag. Carefully squeeze finger-length dough onto a cookie sheet. Use a dull side of butter knife to carve lines into each finger—knuckles and wrinkles. Use an almond to make a fingernail impression at the tip of each finger cookie. Bake the cookies according to the package directions. After baking, "glue" an almond to each finger.

Monstermallows

Frightfully fun treats to eat and to share!

You'll need:
- Marshmallows
- Green food coloring paste
- Chocolate chips
- Small round candies for eyes
- Thin pretzel sticks
- Craft sticks
- New paintbrushes
- Foam cups

Insert a craft stick up through the bottom of a marshmallow so that the marshmallow rests on top of the stick forming a "head". Paint the entire marshmallow green with the green food coloring paste. In a microwave safe bowl, melt the chocolate chips. Dip the top of the marshmallow into the chocolate to create his "hair".

Insert the sticks into the bottom of a foam cup. Place the cup and marshmallow stick into the refrigerator for few minutes to harden the chocolate. Next, dip two round candies into the melted chocolate and "glue" them to the head for eyes. Paint on a chocolate mouth. Break off the ends of a pretzel stick. Poke one piece into each side of the monster's head. Wrap each Monstermallow in cellophane or plastic wrap to give away as treats.

Worms on a Bun

Hot dogs never looked so bad but tasted so good!

You'll need:
- Hot dogs
- Hamburger buns
- Ketchup

Cut the hot dogs into thin slices. Boil or microwave until the slices curl like wiggly worms. Serve three or four worms on a hamburger bun. Add a few squiggles of ketchup.

Egg Eyeballs

So you're not a brain surgeon! How about an eye doctor with eye-popping treats?

You'll need:
- 6 Eggs, hard-cooked, cooled and peeled
- 6-oz container of whipped cream cheese
- 12 Green olives stuffed with pimientos
- Ketchup

Cut the eggs in half widthwise. Remove the yolks and fill the hole with cream cheese.

Press an olive into each cream cheese eyeball, pimiento up, for an eerie green iris and red pupil. Dip a toothpick into ketchup and draw broken blood vessels in the cream cheese!

Boogers on a Stick

The name says it all! Kids will love them!

You'll need:
- 8-oz jar of processed cheese spread
- 3 or 4 drops green food coloring
- 3 dozen pretzel sticks

Melt the processed cheese spread in the micro-wave according to jar directions. Allow the cheese to cool slightly in the jar. Carefully stir in food coloring using just enough to turn the cheese a pale, snot green color. To form boogers: Dip and twist the tip of each pretzel stick into the cheese, lift out, wait twenty seconds, then dip again. When cheese lumps reach a boogerish size, set boogered pretzels on wax paper to cool.

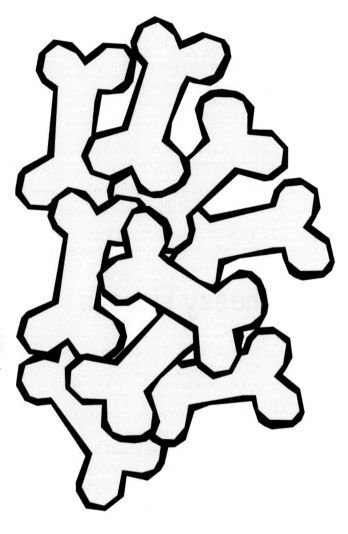

Bone Sandwiches

Who knew it was so easy to make human bones—complete with the marrow and blood!

You'll need:
- White bread
- Peanut butter
- Jelly

Cut the crusts off of several slices of white bread. Spread peanut butter and jelly on the bread. Roll the sandwiches up. You have bones with blood and marrow for dinner!

Bone Bread

And just where did these fresh bones come from?

You'll need:
- Refrigerated bread dough
- Coarse sea salt

Unroll a tube of refrigerated bread dough. Separate the rectangular pieces. Stretch one piece of dough. Carefully cut a slit in the center of each end. Roll and shape the four flaps of dough into knobs that look like the ends of a bone. Repeat with the remaining rectangular pieces of dough. Place the dough bones on an ungreased baking sheet. Sprinkle the bones with coarse sea salt and bake until they are light golden brown.

RECIPES

Chopped Off Fingers Pizza

Make the next homemade pizza one to remember with these misplaced fingertips.

You'll need:
- 1 Red bell pepper
- Mozzarella sticks
- Baked pizza crusts
- Pizza sauce

Core, stem and seed, and cut a red pepper lengthwise into 1-inch wide strips. Cut each strip crosswise into ½-inch pieces. Trim one end to make the fingernails.

Make fingers by cutting each cheese stick in half crosswise. Cut out a ½-inch square notch on the rounded end of each "finger" into which a pepper piece will fit to make a fingernail.

Prepare your homemade pizza crust, sauce, and toppings. Lay several cheese fingers well apart on the crust. Place a red pepper fingernail onto each. Bake as directed.

Cheesy Fingers

You'll need:
- Mozzarella string cheese
- Green pepper
- Cream cheese

Cut each string cheese in half. Carve a shallow area for a fingernail. Carve out tiny wedges to create the knuckle. Cut small strips of green or red peppers. Then cut the strips into fingernail-size pieces. Stick the fingernails to the cheesy fingers with dabs of cream cheese.

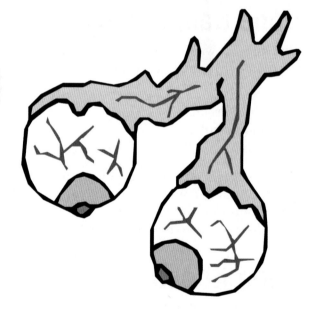

Baked Eyeballs

Keep a close eye on these simple treats.

You'll need:
- Mashed potatoes
- Sliced black olives or round candies

Roll mashed potatoes into eyeball-size balls. Bake them about 20 minutes in a 200° oven—until they are lightly brown and crunchy. Remove the eyeballs from the oven and carefully insert the pupil—sliced black olives or a colorful round candy.

Fruity, Skewered Eyeballs

Who knew eyeballs were so healthy?

You'll need:
- 6 Green grapes
- 6 Raisins
- ½-Cup whipped topping
- 6 Toothpicks
- Oranges

Carefully place a grape onto a toothpick, so that about 1/8-inch of the toothpick comes through the other side of the grape. Place a raisin on the exposed toothpick. Using the backside of a spoon, cover the grape with whipped topping for the "whites" of the eyes! To serve, slice an orange in half. Place the flat side down on a plate and stick the long end of toothpicks into the rind. Garnish the plate with loose grapes.

Frog's Eye Salad

Every little witch and goblin will savor this tasty treat.

You'll need:
- 1 Cup Acini De Pepe—very small round pasta balls
- 2 Cups mandarin oranges
- 1 Cup crushed pineapple
- 1-½ Cups miniature marshmallows
- 3 egg yolks
- 1 Cup sugar
- 1 Tub of whipped topping

Cook the pasta according to the package instructions until tender, but not soft. Drain and rinse the pasta. Drain cans of pineapple and mandarin oranges, reserving the juice. Mix the juices, sugar, and egg yolks in a medium saucepan. Bring the mixture to a full boil. Pour the mixture over the pasta. Refrigerate the pasta overnight. When cooled, mix in the pineapple and oranges. Then fold in the whipped cream and marshmallows.
Chill before serving.

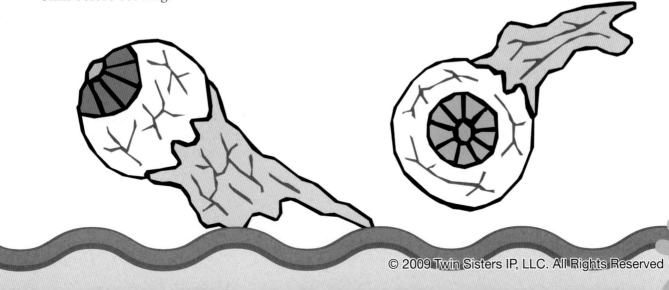

Miniature Tombstones

Your friends are certain to R.I.P. with these simple treats.

You'll need:
- Icing
- Square or rectangle shaped cookies or biscuits
- Water

In a small bowl add small amounts of hot water to the icing, until the mixture becomes fairly runny. Dip each cookie or biscuit into the mixture. Place the cookies onto a foiled tray. Use a toothpick to carve R.I.P. or some other epitaph into the icing. Place the tombstones in the refrigerator for several hours.

Simple Pimples

Go ahead and squeeze these pimples!

You'll need:
- 1-2 dozen cherry tomatoes
- Flavored soft cream cheese spread

Core each tomato with a carrot peeler or small kitchen knife. Drain excess tomato juice. Using a butter knife, fill holes in tomatoes with cream cheese. Gently squeeze each pimple and arrange on a platter.

English Mummies

Imagine who might be behind these tasty wrappings!

You'll need:
- English muffins
- Pizza sauce
- Olive slices
- Green or red pepper pieces
- String cheese (pulled apart)

Split and toast an English muffin. Spread pizza sauce onto one half of the muffin. For eyes, place two olive slices topped with red or green pepper pieces. To make the mummy wrappings, lay strips of string cheese across the muffin. Bake at 350° for about 10 minutes, or until the cheese is melted.

Brain Bread

Adding Brain Bread to your diet will make you very smart!

You'll need:
- ½-Cup (1 stick) unsalted butter
- ½-Cup milk
- ½-Cup water
- 5 to 5-½-Cups all-purpose flour
- 2 Packages dry yeast
- 1 teaspoon salt
- 1 Tablespoon whole anise seed
- 1 Cup sugar
- 4 Eggs
- ⅓-Cup freshly squeezed orange juice
- 2 Tablespoons grated orange zest

In a saucepan heat the butter, milk, and water until the butter melts. In a large mixing bowl, combine 1-½ cups of the flour, the yeast, salt and anise seed, and ½-cup of the sugar. Add the butter and milk mixture and stir until well combined. Add the eggs and beat in 1 cup of flour. Continue to add more flour until the dough is soft but not sticky. Knead the dough on a lightly floured board for 10 minutes, or until smooth and elastic. Lightly grease a large mixing bowl and place the dough in it. Cover with plastic wrap and let rise in a warm place until it doubles in size, about 1-½ hours. Punch the dough down and shape into 2 loaves that look like a brain or skull. Allow the bread to rise in a warm place for 1 hour. Preheat the oven to 350° F. Bake the loaves on a baking sheet for 40 minutes, or until the tops are golden brown.

While the bread is baking, prepare the glaze. In a small saucepan, mix the remaining ½-cup of sugar, orange juice, and orange zest over high heat. Bring to a boil, stirring constantly, for two minutes, then remove from the heat. Keep warm. While the bread is hot, apply the warm glaze to the hot loaves with a pastry brush.

Worm Burgers

These aged, wormy burgers are certain to get a reaction from unsuspecting dinner guests!

You'll need:
- 1-½ Cups Bean Sprouts
- 1-lb Ground beef
- 1 Egg
- Salt and pepper to taste
- Mayonnaise, ketchup, mustard
- Hamburger buns

Wash the bean sprouts with warm water. Mix 1 cup of bean sprouts, ground beef and raw egg together in a bowl. Save the remaining sprouts until later. With adult help, form the burgers into patties, season, and cook them as usual. When they're cooked through, place each on an open bun and sprinkle the remaining "worms" on top. Don't forget the pus and blood on the side—ketchup, mustard, mayonnaise mixed together!

Dinner in a Pumpkin

A delicious hot dish served in a real baked pumpkin!

You'll need:
- 1 Small to medium pumpkin
- 1 4-oz can sliced mushrooms, drained
- 1 Onion, chopped
- 1 10-oz can cream of chicken soup
- 2 Tablespoons vegetable oil
- 1 8-oz can sliced water chestnuts, drained
- 1-½ to 2 lbs ground beef
- 1-½ cups cooked rice
- 2 Tablespoons soy sauce
- 2 Tablespoons brown sugar

Cut off top of pumpkin and clean out the seeds and pulp. Draw an appropriate face on front of pumpkin with permanent marker. In a large skillet, sauté the onion in oil until tender; add meat and brown. Drain drippings from skillet. Add soy sauce, brown sugar, mushrooms and soup; simmer 10 minutes, stirring occasionally. Add cooked rice and water chestnuts. Spoon the mixture into pumpkin shell. Replace the pumpkin top and place entire pumpkin, with filling, on a baking sheet. Bake for 1 hour in 350° oven or until inside meat of pumpkin is tender. Put pumpkin on a plate; remove top and serve.

Cheesy Candy Corn

A hot and tasty take on the traditional Halloween candy.

You'll need:
- Small, round prebaked pizza crusts
- Variety of sliced cheeses: Mozzarella, Provolone, Monterey Jack, Cheddar

Heat the oven to 450° F. Cut small round prebaked pizza crusts into wedges—the shape of a candy corn. Top each wedge with rows of white, orange, and yellow cheeses. Bake the wedges on a cookie sheet for 8 to 10 minutes. Allow the cheesy candy corns to cool for 5 minutes before serving.

Cadaver Dip

Force your guests to do surgery with this frightening but tasty dip.

You'll need:
- Your favorite cheese dip—pliable for molding
- Very thinly sliced cooked ham
- Crackers

On a platter carefully shape your favorite cheese dip into the size and shape of a small human head. Sculpt a nose, lips, and recesses for the eyes. Next, carefully cover the entire sculpture with very thin—almost paper-like—slices of cooked ham. Serve the face dip with crackers.

Fried Spiders

Hot, crunchy munchies!

You'll need:
- 1 Frozen ready-to-bake breaded cream-cheese-filled jalapeno popper
- 4 Frozen ready-to-bake breaded onion rings
- Egg wash
- Wooden toothpicks soaked in water

Thaw the jalapeno poppers and onion rings slightly. Cut the onion rings in half to make the curved legs. Attach the 8 legs to the jalapeno pepper body with egg wash and hold in place with the wet toothpicks. Bake in the oven according to the jalapeno popper package instructions. Carefully arrange on a serving platter—removing the toothpicks.

Wormy Baked Apples

A perfect treat on a cold, damp Halloween night!

You'll need:
- 12 Large baking apples
- 8-oz jar boysenberry or dark colored jam
- 4 Tablespoons butter
- 12 Gummy worm candies

Preheat oven to 350° F. Core apples from the stem end to ½-inch from the bottom. Do not push through. Stuff each hole with 1 teaspoon each of jam and butter. Place in a pan and bake uncovered for 35 to 45 minutes, depending on the size of the apples. Each apple should be tender but not mushy. Remove the apples from the oven and allow to cool 15 minutes. Place each apple in a bowl and spoon syrup from the baking pan around it. Insert a gummy worm in the top of each apple.

Scrambled Scarecrow

Serve guests what's left of your favorite Halloween scarecrow!

You'll need:
- 3 Cups small pretzels
- 3 Cups shoestring potatoes
- 3 Cups Spanish peanuts
- ½ Cup seasoned croutons
- 4-½ oz can French fried onions
- ½ Cup margarine
- ½ Cup Parmesan cheese

Mix all the ingredients in a large baking pan. Bake at 250 degrees for 1 hour, stirring often.

Barf Dip

Tasty and disgusting—a great combination!

You'll need:
- 1 Can of Black beans, drained
- 1 Can of corn, drained
- 1 Jar processed cheese spread
- Diced tomatoes
- Green onions, chopped
- Black olives, chopped
- Tortilla chips

In a microwave-safe bowl, mash ½ can of black beans. Add a small jar of processed cheese spread or cheese dip, some diced tomatoes, drained canned corn, green onions, a few chopped black olives, or any other ugly looking foods. Heat the mixture in the microwave for two or three minutes, stirring frequently. Serve the barf dip with tortilla chips or cut veggies.

Mashed Potato Caterpillars

Caterpillars, maggots—you decide!

You'll need:
- 4 Cups prepared mashed potatoes (your favorite recipe or instant)
- Yellow liquid food coloring
- Red liquid food coloring
- Frozen vegetables: green beans, carrots, corn, peas
- Celery

In a medium mixing bowl, add yellow food coloring to the potatoes and stir to combine; add a few drops of red food coloring to the potatoes and stir again to mix the colors. Continue to add more red or yellow coloring to achieve the desired shade of orange. Using clean, damp hands form the potatoes into small balls, each about 1-½ inches in diameter. On microwave-safe plate, arrange 8 potato balls, side-by-side and overlapping each other slightly, to form curved caterpillar body. Insert green beans for legs on the sides of the caterpillar bodies. Decorate each caterpillar with additional vegetables: thawed frozen carrot cubes, kernels of corn, frozen peas for eyes, a slice of celery for a mouth. Reheat the caterpillars in the microwave and serve.

PUMPKIN CARVING INSTRUCTIONS

1. Draw and cut a lid

Draw a lid on top of your pumpkin. Very carefully cut along the lines with a pumpkin carving saw (available at Halloween stores or discount stores). Angle the blade towards the center of the pumpkin. This creates a ledge to support the lid.

2. Clean and scrape

Clean out the seeds and strings with a scraper or kitchen spoon. Scrape out the inner pulp until the pumpkin wall is approximately 1" thick.

3. Attach the pattern

Copy your pattern, trim the pattern leaving a ½-inch border around the design. Place the pattern on the pumpkin. Press, crease, and fold the pattern so that it fits smoothly against the pumpkin. Tape the pattern to your pumpkin.

4. Transfer the pattern

Ultimately, all the black areas of the pattern will be removed from the pumpkin. Transfer the pattern by poking holes along the edges of the black areas of the pattern with a small, sharp pointed tool. You're creating a dot-to-dot pattern on the pumpkin.

5. Carve the design

Hold the pumpkin in your lap. Hold the pumpkin carving saw like a pencil. Carefully saw dot-to-dot. Saw at a 90° angle to the pumpkin, with gentle pressure and an up and down motion. Work slowly. Pull the saw out completely and reinsert it to change the direction of the cut line. Push the cut piece out with your finger; do not pull the piece out with the blade. Remember that all the black areas of the pattern will be removed from the pumpkin.

Photocopy your pattern
before using!

Photocopy your pattern
before using!

Photocopy your pattern
before using!

Photocopy your pattern
before using!

Photocopy your pattern
before using!

Photocopy your pattern
before using!

Photocopy your pattern
before using!

Photocopy your pattern
before using!

PUMPKIN CARVING PATTERNS

Photocopy your pattern
before using!

Photocopy your pattern
before using!

Photocopy your pattern
before using!

Photocopy your pattern
before using!

Photocopy your pattern before using!

Photocopy your pattern
before using!

Photocopy your pattern
before using!

Photocopy your pattern
before using!

Photocopy your pattern
before using!

Photocopy your pattern
before using!

Photocopy your pattern
before using!

Photocopy your pattern
before using!

Photocopy your pattern
before using!

Sock Wrestling

Mark off a small play area. Players take their shoes off, pull a sock off slighty, and sit around the ring. The idea of the game is for players to somehow remove a sock from their opponents. It can be played one-on-one or with several players in the ring at the same time. Players who lose a sock have to leave the ring.

Witchy Wart

You'll need:
  • A large poster or decoration of a Halloween witch
  • Bubble gum or chewing gum for each player
  • Blindfolds

Hang a picture or decoration of an old Halloween witch on a door or wall. Give each player a piece of gum to chew. Blindfold each player, spin around, and have him or her stick their wad of gum on the witch. The winner is the one who gets the gum "wart" on her nose.

Pumpkin Leg Toss

You'll need:
  • A small pumpkin for each team

Players lay on their backs on the floor right next to each other. One player's head should be next to the next player's feet and so on down the line. Set a small pumpkin on the player's legs at the end of the row. The players try to pass the pumpkin down the row using only their legs and their feet.

Zombie Tag

Mark off a play area, indoors or outdoors. This game follows the classic rules of *Marco Polo*. One player is the Zombie and is blindfolded. The Zombie wanders around the playing area with his or her arms outstretched trying to tag players. When the Zombie groans all the players must groan back and extend their arms. Tagged players are out of the game. The winner is the last player not tagged.

Halloween Pumpkin Hunt

You'll need:
- 10 miniature white pumpkins
- 10 miniature orange pumpkins
- 10 miniature gourds
- Optional: yellow, white and orange construction paper & scissors
- Black felt tip marker

Purchase ten white miniature pumpkins, ten orange miniature pumpkins, and ten miniature gourds. Using a black marker, write the number 1 on the backs of the white pumpkins. Write the number 5 on the backs of the orange pumpkins. Write the number 10 on the backs of the gourds. Hide the pumpkins and gourds around the playing area. Players race to find as many of the pumpkins and gourds before you say "Stop!" Each player adds up the number of points written on the gourds and pumpkins they found. The player with the most points wins. Another option is to use construction paper cut-outs.

Pumpkin Bowling

You'll need:
- Several 2-liter soda bottles
- Water
- Small pumpkins
- Candy prizes

Wrap 2-liter bottles with large white construction paper and decorate them to look like spooky ghosts. Fill the bottles with enough water to weigh them down and stand them like skittles. Player use small pumpkins to bowl at the "ghosts." Give candy prizes for each ghost that is knocked over.

Pass The Witch's Broom

You'll need:
- A broom
- Halloween or party music

Players stand in a circle and pass a broom around while the music is playing. When the music stops the player holding the broom is out of the game. Play until one player remains.

Monster Statues

You'll need:
- Halloween music or party songs

Players stomp and dance around like monsters while the music plays. When the music stops players must freeze. Any player caught moving is out of the game and helps to judge the next round.

Halloween Sticker Stalker

You'll need:
- One sheet of Halloween Stickers for each player

Give each guest a pack/sheet of 10 Halloween stickers. The object of the game is to get rid of all your stickers by sticking them on the other guests. However, if the guest you are "stickering" catches you, he/she gets to stick one of his/her stickers on you. If you are "caught", you must temporarily take your sticker back, and you can try to sticker that same person later. The first one to get rid of all 10 of their stickers wins.

Spider Obstacle Course

Ahead of time, set up an obstacle course with objects to step over, go around, even duck under. Divide into teams each with four players. Team members form spiders by standing together backs facing inward, holding hands with the player directly behind them, and connecting them as a group of four. On "Go!" each group must make it through an obstacle course without disconnecting hands. If the hands come apart, the spider must return to the beginning and start again.

Bug Hunt

You'll need:
- Bag of big plastic bugs
- Flashlight for each player (or at least one for every two players)
- Halloween treat bag for each player (or two-person team)

Hide all the bugs around the room or party area—outside if possible. If indoors, turn off the lights; players or teams use a flashlight to hunt for the bugs in the dark. Search outside after dark. Give prizes to those who find the most bugs!

Spider Web

You'll need:
- A ball of yarn for each player
- Halloween Music

Give each player a ball of yarn. Players tie one end of the yarn loosely around their waist and then stand in a circle. Play your favorite Halloween music CD. Whenever the music stops, players toss their ball of yarn to anyone in the circle. Then, each player wraps the yarn around any part of his or her body—around their leg, arm, waist, foot, fingers, but not around the neck. Play the music again, tossing the yarn to another player when the music stops. Continue until players run out of yarn. There are no winners or losers, and players will be entertained for quite a long time. Plus, they'll have fun untangling themselves.

Belching Contest

Players try burping as many letters in the alphabet as they can. Whoever makes it the furthest through the alphabet wins! Give prizes for the loudest burps, softest burps, most disgusting burps…

Face to Face

Choose one player to stand in the center, while the other players stand in a large circle face-to-face with a partner. The player in the middle calls out commands such as "Face to face," "Back to back," "Side to side." Players take these positions accordingly. When the person in the middle calls "All change!" all the players must find a new partner! The person in the middle tries to get a partner, too. The person left without a partner becomes the new person in the middle and starts to give commands.

Poor Kitty

No one will be able to keep a straight face for very long with this silly game. Players sit on the floor in a circle. Choose one player to be the Poor, Poor Kitty. The Poor, Poor Kitty goes up to another player in the circle purring and meowing, acting like a cat. The friend must pat the kitty on the head and say, "Poor, Poor Kitty" without laughing. If the player laughs, then he or she must become the kitty and try to make another player in the circle laugh.

Ghost Catcher 1

You'll need:
- Large cardboard carton with closable flaps
- Hair dryer
- White foam packing worms
- Scissors
- Timer

Ahead of time, cut an arm-size hole in one side of the cardboard box, near the bottom. Cut a second hole in the bottom of the box, opposite the arm hole, to accommodate the spout of the hair dryer. Fill the carton with about 100 foam packing worms—the ghosts. Close the top of the carton. To play, plug the hair dryer in, set the temperature setting of the hair dryer on Cool, and insert the blower end through the hole cut for it in the bottom of the carton. Turn the hair dryer on so that the ghosts are "flying" around inside the carton. Players take turns putting one arm through the hole in the bottom of the carton, trying to catch the "ghosts". See how many ghosts each player can catch in one minute. Return the ghosts to the carton for the next player's turn.

Ghost Catcher 2

You'll need:

- 1 large pumpkin
- Stickers for each player
- Blindfold

Choose one player to be the Ghost Catcher. Divide the other players into teams of ghosts, for example Red Ghosts, Blue Ghosts. Have enough stickers for the team members to have one each of the same sticker. Players stand in a large circle. Place the pumpkin in the middle of the circle and blindfold the Ghost Catcher. Ghosts crawl around the circle on their knees and try to sneak to the middle to put their stickers on the pumpkin. If the Ghost Catcher touches a ghost, the ghost is out of the game. Once a ghost has placed a sticker on the pumpkin, the ghost is out of the game. Continue until all the ghosts are out of the game. The team that has placed the most stickers wins.

Halloween Memory Game

You'll need:

- A variety of small objects such as plastic spider, pumpkin, candy bar, popcorn, small apple, skeleton mini-toy, acorn, plastic teeth
- Large bag or box to hold objects
- Paper and pencil for each player

Place the objects in a large bag or box. Players take turns reaching into the bag or box to feel the objects. Players then write as many objects as they can recognize and recall. When players are finished—or at a set time limit—reveal the objects in the bag. The player with the most correct answers wins.

Mummy Maker

You'll need:
- Rolls of bathroom tissue for each team

Divide players into teams. One player on each team is the mummy and the others wrap the mummy with bathroom tissue paper as fast as possible. Give prizes for the best mummy or have a race for the fastest mummy wrapped.

Scary Message

Players sit in a large circle. Choose one player to begin the game by whispering a short scary message into the ear of the player sitting to the right of them. They are only allowed to whisper the message one time. That player then whispers it to the person on his or her right, on down the line. When the message reaches the end of the line, the message is spoken aloud.

- "The ghastly green ghost groaned loudly from the gray granite gravestone."
- "The wicked witch wailed wildly as she wound her way through the willows."

Zombies

All players sit or lay as motionless and expressionless zombies. The person who is "it" must do whatever they can to make the zombies smile, giggle, or wiggle in any way without touching them! When "It" gets a zombie to smile, wiggle or giggle, that zombie then joins "it" in trying to get others zombies to smile, giggle, or wiggle. The last zombie wins.

Ghost Waiter

Supplies needed:

- Balloon for each team
- Paper plate for each team

Divide into teams. Set up a course for them to race on. Each player must balance a balloon on a paper plate while walking it down the course and back to their team.

Mummy Hands

You'll need:
- A box filled with various individually wrapped candies for each team
- Bathroom tissue paper for each team
- Tape

Ahead of time, prepare crypts for each team—boxes filled with different types of small individually wrapped candies. Players work together to wrap each other's hands with bathroom tissue paper and secure with clear tape. To play, teams line up. The first person in each line runs to the crypt, removes only one piece of candy using his or her mummy wrapped hands only, and runs back to their team. The next player does the same. The team to empty their crypt first is the winner.

Weaving a Scary Tale

You'll need:
- Index cards
- A pen or pencil
- A minute timer.

Write one phrase on each card that would be a scary line for a Halloween story. Players sit in a circle and pass around the deck of cards, face down. Turn down the lights and give each person a flash light to hold under their face as they speak. Each player chooses a card from the deck, reads the phrase out loud, and then talks for 1 minute adding to the story. When the minute is up, the player passes the cards the next person, who picks a card and steers the story in another direction. The game ends when the last person has gone, when the cards run out or when everyone has had enough of it, it's an endless game!

Story starter suggestions:

- One stormy night...
- The coffin lid opened...
- I smelled the most awful smell ever. It was...
- Inside the witches' cauldron, I could see...
- The door creaked open, and I watched the shadow of a...
- Suddenly, the skeleton moved...
- The goblet was filled with blood...
- In the distance I heard the moan, the groaning of...
- I felt something moving on my shoulder, it was...
- Not one, not two, not three, but four ghosts...

Bat Walk

You'll need

- Crepe paper
- Mirror about 6 inches in diameter
- Cardboard
- Tape or tacks

Ahead of time, tape or tack a winding route of crepe paper around the ceiling of your party room or play area. Purchase a mirror about 6 inches in diameter and attach it to a larger piece of cardboard. Players take turns navigating the course by looking down at the mirror and following the route reflected from the ceiling.

Liver Toss

You'll need:
- Thawed beef liver, rinsed well
- A Bucket or witch's cauldron

Set a bucket or a plastic witch's cauldron several feet away from the players. Players take turns tossing the slice of beef liver into the bucket. For more fun, give each player their own slice of liver to hold while waiting for their turn—you'll be surprised by the reactions.

Broomstick relay

You'll need:
- A broom for each team
- An obstacle course

Divide into teams. Players must "ride" on their broomsticks to the end of the course and back again, and then pass the broomstick to the next player in their team. The first team to have all members finish, wins. Design a small obstacle course if you have room: pumpkins to jump over, a dress-up element such as a witch wig and hat to put on before they start, tossing an apple through a hoop, or dropping a plastic frog or snake into a bucket and saying "Abracadabra!"

Ring the Witch Hat

You'll need:
- Large witch hat—available at crafts and discount stores
- Fiberfill or newspaper to make the hat stand up on its own
- Five heavy paper plates
- Scissors

Ahead of time, stuff the witch hat with fiberfill or newspaper to make it stand up straight. Cut the center out of each of the five plates to make five cardboard rings. Players take turns trying to toss the five rings over the point of the witch hat. After each round of play, stand farther away from the hat.

Halloween Bone Hunt

You'll need:

- Bags of small plastic bones—available at discount stores, Halloween supply stores
- Sack for each child

Ahead of time, mark several prize bones with a sticker. Hide all the bones. On 'Go', players hunt for the bones—as in an Easter egg hunt. Give prizes for the most bones collected and for '"prize bones."

Who's The Ghost?

You'll need:
- A large white sheet

Divide your guests into two groups. Take one group outside of the playing area. Place the sheet over one of the players. Guide the ghost back into the room with the rest of his or her group. The other group must guess who the ghost really is.

The Legend Of Herbert Smear . . .

If done well, this classic Halloween sensory experience is always a hit. Ahead of time, prepare what's left of poor Herbert Smear. Place each item in a separate open container. Choose a great story teller to narrate the event—someone who can easily exaggerate and embellish the tale and who can follow the lead provided by your guests' reactions. Blindfold your guests, have them sit in a circle on the floor, and as the narrator shares the gruesome tale, pass the body parts around the circle for each to feel. Or, in the end of a box, cut a hole large enough to reach a hand in; put each item in its own box.

Brains	A head of cauliflower, overcooked and warm; a peeled, squishy tomato
Scrambled Brains	Lumpy cottage cheese
Worms	Live earthworms, or gummy worms
Hair	Corn Silk best to get a few days before the party and let it dry out.
Eyes	Two frozen olives, or peeled grapes
Heart	A large slice of uncooked beef liver
Intestines	Soggy marshmallows strung together for slimy long intestines
Blood	Ketchup thinned with water
Hands	Two wet latex gloves filled with red gelatin
Ears	Large dried apricots
Nose	The end of a pickle or a hot dog, a soft chicken bone or gristle
Bones:	Fresh crisp celery
Barf/Vomit	Chunky salsa and canned corn mixed together
Flesh	Mashed Potatoes topped with potato flakes, add coloring
Teeth	Dried popcorn kernels
Veins	Cooked, cold spaghetti
Maggots	Cooked, cold rice

Soda Roulette

You'll need:
- Several cans of soda
- Towels for clean up

One unlucky friend will experience the soda fizz sensation. Have a can of soda for each player. Vigorously shake one can of soda. Mix the cans up. Each player chooses a can, puts it up to his nose, and on the count of three opens it! The winner will be revealed!

Gross Eating Contest

You'll need:
- Two paper grocery store bags
- Food items that smell or feel gross: raw onions, cold beans, cooked spaghetti, hardboiled eggs, black olives, cheese chunks, lunchmeat
- Blindfolds

Ahead of time, fill two paper grocery bags with food items that smell or feel gross —nothing spoiled! Each bag must have the same items. Suggestions: raw onions, cold beans, cooked spaghetti, hardboiled eggs, black olives, cheese chunks, lunchmeat, etc. Divide your friends or family members into two teams. Blindfold each player. The first player on each team takes one item from the bag, eats it completely, and then passes the bag to the next player. The first team to eat all the food items in the bag is the winner!

Icky Cobwebs

You'll need:
- String
- Scissors
- Tape
- Water

You're sure to scare your guests as they enter into the darkened room. Cut several 4-foot lengths of string and tape them to the ceiling. Just before the guests arrive hold a bowl of water up to the string and get it wet. When your friends enter the room the wet, slimy string will brush across their foreheads.

Worms In A Pie

You'll need:
- Gummy worms
- Whipped topping
- Aluminum pie plates or deep disposable plates—one for each player
- Blindfolds

Place the same amount of gummy worms on each plate and cover with whipped cream. Blindfold each player. On the count of three, each player dips into the pie with their mouths, trying to pull out as many worms as they can. See who can pull out the most worms in a time limit or just set a certain amount of worms to find. For more fun, and if everyone is willing, put all the gummy worms and whipped cream in one large container and let players search together.

Lost Eyeballs

You'll need:
- Marbles
- Medium-sized plastic storage container
- Cooked spaghetti
- Food coloring
- Cooking oil

The lost eyeballs are really marbles! Place the marbles in a medium-size plastic storage container. Fill the container with cooked spaghetti noodles doctored up with a red food coloring and a small amount of cooking oil. Players take turns searching for the lost eyeballs using only their feet.

Monster Soup

You'll need:
- A large bowl
- Cooked oatmeal
- Halloween toys

Fill a large bowl with cooked oatmeal. Chill the oatmeal in the refrigerator. Mix in small plastic Halloween toys like eyeballs, bats, spiders, etc. Players close their eyes and reach into the bowl, and find one toy.

What Smells?

Have fun experimenting with smells! Collect several items that have distinctive smells such as: lemon, orange peel, perfume soaked cotton, banana, pine needles, chocolate, coffee, dirt, vanilla, garlic, onion, mint, vinegar, moth balls, rose petals, saw dust, and pencil shavings. If you're brave enough, add some disgusting smells, too. Keep the items separated and enclosed in plastic containers so that the odors do not mix. Blindfold a friend—or punch holes in the top of the containers to eliminate the need of a blindfold. Can your friends identify each item by smell? Do your friends have an immediate reaction to certain smells? Can they share memories associated with the smell?

Egg Float

You'll need:
- Two large glasses filled with lukewarm water
- ½-Cup Salt
- 1 Egg

Make an egg float and astonish your guests! Thoroughly dissolve about ½-cup of salt in one glass of water. Gather your audience around. Drop the egg into the unsalted water. It will sink to the bottom. Remove the egg and look sad, pretending your experiment never works. Now put the egg into the salt water, and your audience will be amazed to see the egg float.

Eyeball Relay

You'll need:
- 1 Ping pong ball for each team (painted like an eyeball)
- 1 Spoon for each team

Divide players into teams. Give the first person on each team a spoon and a ping pong ball. Set up the course to where they have to carry the "EYE" on the spoon to the end of the course and come back. Hand off to the next player and continue until all team members have run the course. First team done wins!

Worm Feast

You'll need:
- Canned Spaghetti for each player
- Small bowl for each player
- Blindfold for each player
- Bib for each player
- Towels for cleanup

Select any number of players. Tie a bib around each player's neck. Blindfold each player. Bring out a small bowl of cold canned spaghetti—for more fun use food coloring to make the spaghetti look more revolting. Show the onlookers and encourage a strong reaction: "Oh, grossssssss!" Then, on "Go!" players eat their worms as quickly as possible, using only their mouths— no hands. The player to finish the worm feast first, wins.

Homemade Boogers

You'll need:
- Small bowl
- Craft glue
- Warm water
- Green food coloring
- Borax® Laundry booster
- Clean, empty 16-oz plastic bottle with lids

In a small bowl mix together ½-cup each of craft glue and warm water. Add drops of green food coloring until the boogers look green enough! Set the boogers aside for a moment. Put ½-cup of Borax® laundry booster (available at most grocery and discount stores) in a clean, empty 16-oz plastic soda bottle. Fill the bottle with the water, replace the lid, and shake it until the powder dissolves. Pour several tablespoons of the solution into the booger mixture and stir until very clumpy. When the boogers are just right, have a booger flicking contest with your friends!

Spider T-Shirts

You'll need:
- An old white t-shirt
- Black and red garment dye
- An old bucket (or one that it's ok if it turns black inside)
- Rubber bands
- Permanent magic marker
- Small paintbrush

Fill a bucket with black dye. Now take an old white t-shirt and put rubber bands in a concentric circle from the middle of the shirt. The more rubber bands you use, the webbier your shirt will look. Submerge the whole t-shirt in the bucket of black dye. and let it dry for 24 hours. When completely dry, remove the rubber bands. Use a permanent marker to draw a spider on the web. Add a bloody touch by dipping a paintbrush into red dye and splattering your shirt.

Spider Bracelets

You'll need:
- Black construction paper
- Scraps of colored construction paper
- Scissors
- Tape
- White crayon
- Pencil

Fold a sheet of black construction paper in half. Along the folded edge, lay your hand palm down midway through your palm and trace your fingers with a white crayon. Cut out the outline of the finger and unfold the paper. You will have a complete image of a spider with eight legs. Turn the spider over and curl the spider's leg by rolling the legs around a pencil. To make the bracelet, cut a 1-inch strip of black paper from the remaining scraps and form it into a circle. Tape the ends together. Attach the bracelet to the underside of the spider using tape or glue. Decorate your spider with wiggle eyes, various shapes cut from different colored construction paper. Slip your wrist through the bracelet.

Skeleton Art

You'll need:
- Black construction paper
- Cotton swabs
- White paper
- Scissors
- Glue

Draw a skeleton skull on the white paper. Cut it out and glue it to a sheet of black construction paper. Using the cotton swabs as bones arrange the skeleton body. Give the skeleton arms, legs, ribs, etc. Cut the cotton swabs into smaller pieces, if necessary.

Glue all the cotton swabs onto the black paper.

Haunted Soles

You'll need:
- Washable white paint
- Sponges or paint brushes
- Black construction paper
- Permanent marker

Coat the bottoms of each guest's feet with white paint. Then they step onto black construction paper. Once dry, add eyes and a mouth with permanent marker or black paint.

Glue Ghosts

You'll need:
- White school glue
- Waxed paper
- Wiggle-eyes
- Felt, buttons, pom-poms, etc (all optional)

Place a piece of waxed paper on a flat surface. Squeeze glue from the bottle into the shape of a ghost. Place wiggle-eyes into the glue. Decorate your ghost with buttons, construction paper, felt, beads, jewels, ribbon, etc. Add a piece of yarn to the top if you plan on hanging your ghost. Allow the ghosts to dry overnight. Once dry carefully peel the ghosts from the waxed paper. Glue the ghosts to craft sticks to make puppets.

Horrible Hands

You'll need:
- Clear plastic gloves (available at beauty supply stores)
- Candy corn
- Cold popcorn
- Yarn

Make these treats ahead of time or set out the supplies and allow your guests to make their own horrible hands! Insert one candy corn at the tip of each finger inside a clear plastic glove, pointy side up, for fingernails. Fill the glove with popcorn and use a piece of yarn to tie a bow at the wrist.

Pumpkin Lantern

You'll need:
- 12" x 18" orange construction paper
- Ruler
- Scissors
- Glue
- Stapler
- 9" x 12" green construction paper
- Red, yellow, and black construction paper scraps
- Pencil

Fold the orange construction paper in half to make a 6" x 18" rectangle. With a ruler, measure 2" in from the open edge and draw an 18" line across the paper. Then draw lines 1-inch apart between the fold of the paper and the 18" line. Cut on the shorter lines, starting at the fold. Unfold the paper, bend it into a cylinder, and paste the side edges together. To make a handle for the lantern, cut 1-½" x 12" strip of green construction paper, staple the strip in an arc to the top edge of the lantern. Glue eyes, a nose and a mouth for the lantern from scraps of red, yellow and black construction paper.

Dangling Donuts

You'll need:
- Donuts
- String
- Clothesline
- Scissors

Ahead of time, tie a clothesline or piece of rope across a doorway or playing area. Tie long pieces of string to donuts. To play, tie the other end of the string to the clothesline or rope so that the donuts are dangling at about chin height to the average player. Hang several donuts at the same time. The object of the game is to see who can eat their swinging donut in the shortest amount of time.

Why did the vampire go to the orthodontist?

To improve his bite

What do you get when you cross a vampire and a snowman?

Frostbite

Why do witches use brooms to fly on?

Because vacuum cleaners are too heavy

Do zombies eat popcorn with their fingers?

No, they eat the fingers separately

Why don't skeletons ever go out on the town?

Because they don't have any body to go out with

What did one ghost say to the other ghost?

"Do you believe in people?"

Why do mummies have trouble keeping friends?

They're so wrapped up in themselves

What type of dog do vampire's like the best?

Bloodhounds

What is a skeleton's favorite musical instrument?

A trombone

Why do vampires need mouthwash?

They have bat breath

What do goblins and ghosts drink when they're hot and thirsty on Halloween?

Ghoul-aid!!!

What is a Mummie's favorite type of music?

Wrap

What's a monster's favorite bean?

A human bean

What do ghosts say when something is really neat?

Ghoul

Why did the game warden arrest the ghost?

He didn't have a haunting license

Why didn't the skeleton dance at the party?

He had no body to dance with

Where does Count Dracula usually eat his lunch?

At the casketeria

What happens when a ghost gets lost in the fog?

He is mist

Why doesn't Dracula mind the doctor looking at his throat?

Because of the coffin

Why is a ghost such a messy eater?

Because he is always a goblin

JOKES

What do you call a goblin who gets too close to a bonfire?

A toasty ghosty

What tops off a ghost's ice cream sundae?

Whipped scream.

What kind of makeup do ghosts wear?

Mas-scare-a.

Why did the skeleton cross the road?

To go to the body shop.

What happens when two vampires meet?

It was love at first bite!

What do you call two spiders that just got married?

Newlywebbed

What did the ghost say to the man at the coffee shop?

Scream or sugar!

Which building does Dracula visit in New York?

The Vampire State Building.

60

What pasta should you eat on Halloween?

Fettucinni Afraid-o

Why didn't the skeleton cross the road?

He had no guts.

Why do vampires scare people?

They are bored to death!

What's it like to be kissed by a vampire?

It's a pain in the neck.

How does a girl vampire flirt?

She bats her eyes.

What is a vampire's least favorite food?

A steak

Why did Dracula go to the dentist?

He had a fang-ache.

Who does Dracula get letters from?

His fang club.

What kind of gum do ghosts chew?

Boo Boo Gum.

Why did Dracula take cold medicine?

To stop his coffin.

How do you keep a monster from biting his nails?

Give him screws.

What can't you give the headless horseman?

A headache.

Why did the headless horseman go into business?

He wanted to get ahead in life.

What's a monsters favorite desert?

I-Scream!!

JOKES

How do witches keep their hair in place while flying?

With scare spray

What kind of streets do zombies like the best?

Dead ends

What is a vampires favorite holiday?

Fangsgiving

Where did the goblin throw the football?

Over the ghoul line

What do you call a witch who lives at the beach?

A sand-witch.

What do birds give out on Halloween night?

Tweets

Why are vampires like false teeth?

They all come out at night

How can you tell a vampire likes baseball?

Every night he turns into a bat

63

How can you tell when a vampire has been in a bakery?

All the jelly has been sucked out of the jelly doughnuts

What's a monster's favorite play?

Romeo and ghouliet

What was the witch's favorite subject in school?

Spelling

Why don't mummies take vacations?

They're afraid they'll relax and unwind

Why did the witch stand up in front of the audience?

She had to give a screech

Where did the goblin throw the football?

Over the ghoul line